Tipton

Tipton Poetry Journal, lo publishes quality poetry fr

Statistics: This issue features 39 poets from the United States (22 different states), and 4 poets from India, Italy, South Korea and Ukraine.

Our Featured Poem this issue is "Picking Up Steam," written by Liz Dolan. Liz's poem, which also receives an award of $25, can be found on page 3. The featured poem was chosen by the Board of Directors of Brick Street Poetry, Inc., the Indiana non-profit organization who publishes *Tipton Poetry Journal*.

Barry Harris reviews *Ticker* by Mark Neely.

Cover Photo: *Harvest Time* by Brendan Crowley.

Barry Harris, Editor

Copyright 2022 by the Tipton Poetry Journal.

All rights remain the exclusive property of the individual contributors and may not be used without their permission.

Tipton Poetry Journal is published by Brick Street Poetry Inc., a tax-exempt non-profit organization under IRS Code 501(c)(3). Brick Street Poetry Inc. publishes the Tipton Poetry Journal, hosts the monthly poetry series *Poetry on Brick Street* and sponsors other poetry-related events.

Contents

Dan Carpenter 1
James Green 2
Liz Dolan 3
Bruce Robinson 4
Gene Twaronite 5
Philip C. Kolin 6
Thomas Alan Orr 8
Richard Schiffman 10
Mykyta Ryzhykh 11
Timothy Pilgrim 12
Rosemary Freedman 14
Hollie Dugas 15
Dave Malone 16
Bart Edelman 17
Karla Linn Merrifield 20
Tara Menon 21
D.C. Buschmann 22
R L Swihart 23
Sophia Upshaw 24
Janelle Finamore 25
Bruce Levine 26
Paul Lojeski 27
Arvilla Fee 28
George Freek 29
Michelle Hartman 30
Michael Lee Johnson 32

Cameron Morse	*33*
Tawn Parent	*34*
Mark Vogel	*36*
Eugene Stevenson	*37*
John Grey	*38*
Bruce Campbell	*40*
Ken Poyner	*42*
Nancy Huxtable Mohr	*43*
Haro Lee	*44*
Katherine Hoerth	*45*
Lynette Lamp	*46*
Alessio Zanelli	*47*
Kit Kennedy	*48*
Tia Paul-Louis	*49*
Ruth Holzer	*50*
Saraswati Nagpal	*51*
Brandon Hansen	*52*
Review: *Ticker* **by Mark Neely**	*54*
Contributor Biographies	*61*

Blood

Dan Carpenter

Larry Smalls was a fighting man
and sure as hell was built for it
even now I'd kill for that body
color of a bruise
shape of a comic book superhero
made not in any gym
but down at the stockyards
in the days they sent cows down a chute
and black men brained them with sledgehammers

all day he'd do this work
then he'd come home and fight
but the muscle was wasted on those battles
his fights were with City Hall, the Man, the System
he took on police brutality with brute force
of a voice unschooled, untrained
raised to a quaint eloquence
by rage over loved ones known and unknown
herded, penned, branded and felled
by detached deciders of their usefulness

some day, I figured, Larry might be among them
for the moment, he swung his hammer
no more conscious of *some day*
than a child

Dan Carpenter has published poetry and fiction in *Illuminations, Pearl, Poetry East, Southern Indiana Review, Maize, Flying Island, Pith, The Laurel Review, Sycamore Review, Prism International, Fiction, Hopewell Review* and other journals. A collection of columns written for *The Indianapolis Star*, where he earned his living, was published by Indiana University Press in 1993 with the title *Hard Pieces: Dan Carpenter's Indiana*. Dan has published two books of poems, *The Art He'd Sell for Love* (Cherry Grove, 2015) and *More Than I Could See* (Restoration, 2009); and two books of non-fiction.

The Orionids
James Green

are lonely like the rest of us. They fall
from Orion, that hapless hunter
immortalized in the nightscape
where he finds his final peace,

so I wake early and walk into darkness
to pay homage, and I wait for his star-sparks
to follow some tender urge. But now the sky
is indifferent. Clouds of a nameless color

smear the southern horizon and I wonder
what it means that I would come to this place
in the steep of darkness for companionship,
to meet a hero who hides in clouds.

Sitting on a lawn chair, under a blanket,
hands cupping a mug of coffee, I notice
clouds beginning to drift and the dog star
peek into view, then disappear again.

I will comb the morning for metaphor.

James Green has worked as a naval officer, deputy sheriff, high school English teacher, professor of education, and administrator in both public schools and universities. Recipient of two Fulbright grants, he has served as a visiting scholar at the University of Limerick in Ireland and the National Chung Cheng University in Taiwan. In addition to academic publications, including three books, Green is the author of three chapbooks of poetry and a fourth, *Long Journey Home*, is forthcoming after winning the Charles Dickson Chapbook Contest sponsored by the Georgia Poetry Society., Individual poems have appeared in literary magazines in England, Ireland, and the United States. He resides in Muncie, Indiana.

Picking Up Steam
Liz Dolan

My father was a car knocker,
the handmaiden of the locomotive
as it rested, sweated in Oak Point Yard, xx
en route to Hartford and New Haven.

After his calloused fingers secured
her pistons, bolts, and screws,
he'd rap his iron wrench
on her corrugated door signaling
her safety to the engineer.

Royal, magisterial, her black-velvet flanks
illuminated by the fat summer moon,
she'd snort smoke, whistling her high soprano,
Tirnagog kicking up pebbles,
looping the American miles.
And my father, an immigrant,
ebonized by her grease,
a part of it, a part of it, a part of it.

A nine time Pushcart nominee in both prose and poetry, **Liz Dolan** has published two poetry collections. Her ten grandchildren pepper her life. Liz lives in Rehobeth Beach, Delaware.

Matters of Significant Portent
Bruce Robinson

Meanwhile, nobody's talking about the weather.
Yes, there are plenty of books overdue at the library.
Have you been to the grocery store recently? Prices
are insane! Yes, I know there's a
crisis somewhere overseas, but somewhere else
doctors think they've discovered how to
commiserate with a heretofore
incurable disease. Don't let me forget

I slept through the super bowl's halftime show;
let's not even talk about how much it costs
to fill up the car; I know I'm upset
each time I drive to the mall, but is it
really all that big a deal? You know
it's supposed to snow big-time tonight?

Recent work by **Bruce Robinson** appears or is forthcoming in *Tar River Poetry, Spoon River, Rattle, Mantis, Two Hawks Quarterly, Peregrine, Tipton Poetry Journal, North Dakota Quarterly,* and *Aji*. He lives in Brooklyn, New York.

Tracks in the Surf
Gene Twaronite

Can you read this? Most days, my words look more like tracks of a sandpiper skittering along the edge of the sea. But I see them clearly now—o blessed words! There's so much I want to say before they leave me again and I must go back to that inarticulate cell, as memories play out like silent movies, and I must watch them speechless. Moving in and out on the stage, strange people arrive, imploring me to do things, uttering sounds and looking at me as if I'm supposed to understand them. They start off smiling, but then begin to frown. Their voices grow louder, and I can feel their frustration slowly rise in an angry wave. *Why can't you understand me? Don't you remember?* Sometimes they yell at me, and all I can do is babble. But I must hurry. The words are fleeting, and I must write while I can. So if you're still here, please share this with that lady with the luminous face. She's here every morning. When she smiles, she fills my every dark corner, and her words play softly on my soul. Sometimes she opens a book, and points to the tracks on the page as she speaks. And each night before I go to sleep, she sings to me a sad song that reminds of what I do not know. Please, tell her that I ….

Gene Twaronite is the author of four collections of poetry as well as the rhyming picture book *How to Eat Breakfast*. His first poetry book *Trash Picker on Mars*, published by Kelsay Books, was the winner of the 2017 New Mexico-Arizona Book Award for Arizona poetry. His newest poetry collection *Shopping Cart Dreams* will be published by Kelsay Books in 2022. Gene's poems have been described as: "ranging from edgy to whimsical to inscrutable … playfully haunting and hauntingly playful." A former New Englander, Gene now lives in Tucson. Follow more of his poetry at genetwaronite.poet.com or
https://www.instagram.com/genetwaronitepoetry/.

The Spanish Lady
Philip C. Kolin

New York City, Winter 1918

We lived in a tenement where half the doors
were draped with black crepe. Long coughing
spells carried down the hallways, stoked
by the coal-less chill. The city was saturated

with colds. Fines were issued for spitting
on the sidewalk. Hearses trotted past
our windows hour after hour. Nights
we left the windows open to kill the germs.

Masked mail carriers looked like ghosts.
The Spanish Lady killed more of our soldiers
than the Germans had. We wore red
because the flu didn't like that color,

and left slice onions out at night to keep
from getting sick. We quaffed Pluto Water
to wash out germs, even if it killed you.
We too were on a death watch: our own.

Monkey Grass
Philip C. Kolin

She planted monkey grass all up and
down her steep driveway each spring.
It was her green menagerie.

Her plant keeper outfit included large
swaths of sweat just underneath
a large straw hat, the fringe extending

into the cloudless sky surrounding her.
She joked the grass marked the border
between her house and heaven's gate.

It happily endured generations of kids'
bikes, drivers and their hurrying, crushing
tires, and the scorching Mississippi sun

that tried to wilt it brown.
But it survived many seasons because
of her watering and pruning; it even stood

in a strong wind. But then she was gone,
and relatives forgot the monkeys; but their
drooping crowns looked like sad straw hats.

Philip C. Kolin is the distinguished Professor of English Emeritus at the University of Southern Mississippi. He has published over 40 books including 14 collections of poetry, the most recent being *Americorona* (Wipf & Stock, 2021).

Roofer

Thomas Alan Orr

I ain't first class but I ain't white trash ~ Tom Petty

Pouring a shot of Jack into his beer,
he has no use, he says, for a band
without pedal steel and no time
for women who haven't read Steinbeck,
with whom conversation is like carrying
a bundle of shingles up a ladder in high heat.

He sometimes regrets his dilatory ways —
those hungover mornings that cost him more jobs
than he cares to count, though when he works
he keeps up with the Mexicans, who can lay
ten squares each on a good day in blazing sun,
his burnished skin as dark as theirs.

They call him *Blanco y Negro*.
He banters with them in broken Spanish,
sharing their simple fare of beans and rice
and warm tortillas under the trees in August,
attending baptisms and *quinceañeras*
like the crazy *tio* everybody loves.

That day haunts him — when he and Paco
straddled the ridge line and Paco stood
and suddenly pitched over, falling two stories
to the ground. He sees Paco in his dreams,
dancing fearlessly on the roof, reaching
for the sky and laughing in the summer sun.

He wonders, if not for a two-beer buzz
at lunch, could he have been quicker,
grabbing Paco's leg or arm in time?
As if to atone, on *Día de los Muertos*
he makes the trip alone to the cemetery
in Juarez to light a candle at the grave.

Roofers, he says, with a rueful smile,
are closer to heaven than most —
a good thing given a trade that gets
no respect until the rain is falling
on your baby's head and the roofers
come and the world is safe again.

Lazarus Jones Keeps a Butterfly in Winter

Thomas Alan Orr

On a warm September day she flew
like summer's last breath through an open window
in the upstairs room where he kept Kia's things –
hairbrush on the dresser, a book of poems,
framed picture of them together
on a porch swing in a sweeter time.

He was in the seat of the old International,
which croaked and spit before stalling
in the yard. He muttered, gazed heavenward,
and saw the Painted Lady let herself in.
The night turned cold, the window closed.
He put out a dish of juice and she drank deeply.

Fall gave way to winter and still she thrived.
He named her Vanessa for the genus, *Vanessa cardui*,
and watched her flitter about the room,
colors bright – forewing olivescent, ochreous, brown –
backwing transversely marbled – marvelous!
How much, he wondered, can she know?

She was alone in her wildness, like Lazarus himself,
twice alone, losing Kia, being the only black farmer
in the township. He could have left,
but farming was all he ever knew. And so
he sought consolation in Vanessa's company.
She alit upon his arm, antennae stroking him.

In spring, the window open, she circled once
around the room as if to say farewell
and, like the Holy Ghost, touched his head
before she fluttered free, diaphanous
in a shaft of sunlight, as if inviting him
to come forth into the newness of the world.

Thomas Alan Orr's most recent collection is *Tongue to the Anvil: New and Selected Poems* (Restoration Press). His work has appeared in numerous journals. He works for a community development organization in Indianapolis and lives on a small farm in Shelby County where he raises Flemish Giant rabbits.

Encouraged
Richard Schiffman

I spent the morning hiding in a thicket
where you couldn't find me even if you tried.
True, that world-meanderer, the breeze,
sniffed me out. But its lips are sealed.

When I spoke by rote my old man woes,
the backlit gasses trembled with consternation.
You are as green as you want to be, they insisted,
you are our own two-legged emanation.

My legs are bowed, I told the crow that had
the sky entire to fly through. Caw, caw, he said,
you are not dead, you can take flight
where you are sitting.

The sun concurred, it lit my face.
It burned away my hang-dog resignation.
I wore that light of day all day
until my nightly assignation.

No need to fear the night, night told.
For rest assured, the stars are also suns
that light the way from dusk till dawn.
They've got your back, be bold.

Richard Schiffman is an environmental reporter, poet and author of two biographies based in New York City. His poems have appeared on the BBC and on NPR as well as in *Alaska Quarterly, New Ohio Review, Christian Science Monitor, New York Times, Writer's Almanac, This American Life in Poetry, Verse Daily* and other publications. His first poetry collection *What the Dust Doesn't Know* was published in 2017 by Salmon Poetry.

Before-rain before-fear
Mykyta Ryzhykh

Before-rain before-fear more than the skill before the heart
Anabioses of lame handwriting in the notebook of phobias
Involuntarily the rituals of movements turn into a prayer book of memories
The constant of terrorist attacks of heart contractions
Who will not wake up in the morning next time?
To whom did you extend your logos last night?
Multibillion-dollar humanity
Eons of yawning
Indifferent postcards of tears during the military occupation

a stone is a ruin
Mykyta Ryzhykh

a stone is a ruin
again
a stone is only a ruin

Revenge of madness
Mykyta Ryzhykh

Revenge of madness
Little gophers of construction in the palm of hopes

Guns screamed
The end of all roads
We swam out to drown
The only prospect is waiting

Mykyta Ryzhykh lives in Ukraine and was a finalist of the Crimean fig competition and 2022 Pushcart Nominee (*Tipton Poetry Journal*). Mykyta has been published in the journals *White Mammoth, Soloneba, Littsentr, Plumbum Press, Ukrainian Literary Gazette, Bukovynskyi Journal, Stone Poetry Journal, Tipton Poetry Journal, Alternate route, dyst journal, Better than Starbucks poetry & Fiction Journal, Allegro Poetry Magazine, Littoral Press, Asorn haiku Journal, Book of Matches, Ice Floe Press.*and *Literary Chernihiv.*

Shadow burial
Timothy Pilgrim

Horizon jagged near sundown,
I stop tottered trek, find clearing,
stream, make fire, camp.

With luck, I'll outlast night.
Squawk of jays in tree conjures back
my boyhood life — father of father,

abuelo — his memory flares,
immerses me in what sowed hate.
Not dismissive back of hand,

fast, hard, on pimpled face. Nor scorn
sprayed for chores left undone,
irreverent talk, refusal to pray.

More, ferity seen as I lay tall-grassed
by willows lining bank of creek.
Laddered, high, Abuelo reaches deep

through leaves, magpie nest,
babies, beaks eager to eat —
one by one, strokes each a bit,

rips tiny head off slim black neck.
Blood-spurt memory beset
fifty years hence, I namaste

my wrinkled hands, breathe in,
hum low to bury this shadow.
I forgive him, then forget.

Fear on the way out
Timothy Pilgrim

FOMO, as some would text,
short for Fear Of Missing Out,

has little to do with differences, say,
between prophet — knowing

the end is near — and profit
gained from a lottery win

just before the denouement.
It's more a powerful form of worry —

perhaps about brooding whether one
is a cuckolder of diminutive stature,

giver of lesser heart-panged slights.
Or, akin to Odysseus worrying

if he should choose sirens over home.
Certainly powerful enough

to prompt any stable person to leave
a perfectly good life at halftime.

Timothy Pilgrim, Montana native and Pacific Northwest poet, has a few hundred acceptances from U.S. journals such as *Seattle Review, San Pedro River Review, Tipton Poetry Journal,* and *Santa Ana River Review*, and international journals such as *Windsor Review* and *Toasted Cheese* in Canada, *Prole Press* in the United Kingdom, and *Otoliths* in Australia. He is the author of *Seduced by metaphor* (2021).

To all the people who love wildflowers
Rosemary Freedman

If I were to tell you that
joshua trees write poems about
the shadows made by the rose frost
of your cheeks the color of zinnias.
Your crooked smile is a welcome that
invites the sun through a door of darkness.
An owl lands at your feet, pulling
at the hem of your pants.
All the bright colors
are like fireworks on
an ordinary day.
Indigo baptista,
New England Aster,
Queen Anne's lace,
bachelor buttons.
Redbuckia —
the gold petals glow like
lightening bugs, like masa.
If you wait
for the rain long enough, the wildflowers
will rise like the voices of children
at their first holiday pageant.

Rosemary Freedman is a poet, a painter and an advanced practice nurse. She has 7 children and lives in Noblesville, Indiana with her husband Jack. Rosemary enjoys growing peonies and tending her large garden. She is a graduate of Indiana University. Rosemary is currently working toward her masters of fine arts in poetry at Butler University.

13 Life Lessons from Holden Caufield
Hollie Dugas

1. Song lyrics are better when you mishear them.
2. There isn't a catcher's mitt in the world big enough.
3. Nobody ever got nowhere without a void.
4. Who wants flowers when they're dead?
5. Stuff you'd rather not say is always the stuff worth saying.
6. A red hunting hat will intimidate the dickens out of people.
7. This world is full of creeps and morons.
8. This planet is godforsaken; romanticize everything.
9. Nothing's ever all true.
10. Laugh like the dickens whenever you can.
11. Trouble is, no one will ever truly hear you.
12. I don't know what I mean by that—but I mean it.
13. Did I tell you about the ducks, yet?

Hollie Dugas lives in New Mexico. Her work has been selected to be included in *Barrow Street, Reed Magazine, Crab Creek Review, Redivider, Porter House Review, Pembroke, Salamander, Poet Lore, Watershed Review, Mud Season Review, Little Patuxent Review, The Louisville Review, The Penn Review, Chiron Review, Louisiana Literature,* and *CALYX*. Most recently, her poem was selected as winner of the 22nd Annual Lois Cranston Memorial Poetry Prize at CALYX, in addition to, the 2022 Heartwood Poetry Prize. Hollie has been a finalist twice for the Peseroff Prize at *Breakwater Review*, Greg Grummer Poetry Prize at *Phoebe, Fugue's* Annual Contest, and has received Honorable Mention in *Broad River Review*. Additionally, "A Woman's Confession #5,162" was selected as the winner of *Western Humanities Review* Mountain West Writers' Contest (2017). Recently, Hollie has been nominated for a 2020 Pushcart Prize and for inclusion in Best New Poets 2021. She is currently a member on the editorial board for *Off the Coast*.

Autumn Float

Dave Malone

We make the gravel bar before dusk.
Our kayaks groan with as much
wearied muscle as our own.
Fire is first, and driftwood disappears
in air as blue flame then ash.

We decide against tents,
those nylon slivers made to resist
evening wind and rain.
We would rather face the flood
of stars above the bluff.

After fish and scotch and fire,
sleeping bags form around us
while we chat then stop
because the river shares a secret

in a low constant whoosh
that hushes owl and coyote,
and ushers us
into the arms of slumber.

Poet and filmmaker **Dave Malone** lives in the Missouri Ozarks. His latest poetry volume is *Tornado Drill* (Aldrich Press, 2022), and his poems have appeared in *Plainsongs, San Pedro River Review,* and *Delta Poetry Review.* He can be found online at davemalone.net or via Instagram @dave.malone.

The Tunnel of Love
Bart Edelman

Born in *The Tunnel of Love*—
Palisades Amusement Park, July, 1961.
Mother did not wait for ride's end,
Dispensing me by darkness,
On the metal floor of the car,
Before I could witness light.
The event made national headlines—
Caused quite a stir in the family,
Since Father ran off, hours later,
With a woman who swallowed swords,
And refused to take no for an answer.
I reveal this tidbit of information,
Merely as historical fact alone.

My sudden entrance into calamity,
Came at a costly price—
An admission ticket I've yet to cash,
If I could only gauge its worth.
That I find I'm constantly drawn
To tight quarters and little space,
Should arrive without surprise.
I'm far more comfortable in places
Where others squeal or scream—
Unsure of the destination ahead.
This, then, is cargo I carry;
Safe passage through a curious life.

The Deed
Bart Edelman

No mention of the deed made,
The entire family did its dance—
Over, around, and under it—
As if a prize would be awarded
To the relative who safely skirted
The issue for an additional year.
Surely, Aunt Betty ruled the roost.
Uncle Cliff came prepared with a joke.
Cousin Moe curled up beside the cat,

And Grandpa Ben decided nothing mattered,
Except his devotion to the Cardinals—
Despite their ten-game losing streak.
My mother and father, not to be outdone,
Played gin rummy outside on the veranda,
Drinking quite a few banana daiquiris,
And my sister, Bree, spent an hour or two
Removing all the pickles from a giant jar,
Before replacing them back again—
For some particularly unknown reason—
Being, of course, part of *her condition*.
By the time dinner was served,
Uncle Archie had already departed—
Due to a sudden case of the flu—
And Aunt Lydia realized she needed to bathe,
Come hell or high water, she said.
We consumed what there was of the turkey,
In far less than half an hour,
Escaping yet another holiday—
None the wiser, nor any more deficient.
Later, Bree fell asleep on my shoulder,
In the backseat of the car, halfway home.
Mother and Father spoke in hushed voices
But loud enough, finally, to mention,
Wasn't it great to see everyone again?
I wanted to ask about Dad's brother, Doug—
The guy who robbed the bank outside Detroit
And is stuck in some jail who knows where.
However, I knew it was probably a bad idea
And would hurt Dad more than I thought.
Yeah, fun to see the gang, I replied,
Simply leaving it at that.
Besides, I guess, if I really do want to know
More about the deed from anyone else,
Thanksgiving is only a year away.

The Midway
Bart Edelman

I've tried to find the Midway—
Quite a few times now—
But to no avail, I'm afraid.
It simply evades me, at all cost,
Despite the map I carry
In the chest pocket of my shirt,
Directing me to the very spot
Where the hoopla should occur.

I imagine I must be half the distance
Between the place I began
And the final stop on the line—
Yet no exact measurement exists.
Oddly enough, I remain in limbo,
Going both forward and backward,
Making an appraisal of my situation
A precarious and foolish call.

If I could only reach the Midway—
With its amusements and concessions galore—
This journey would have a purpose;
I might require little more.
Perhaps, what I thought was an end,
May well be dawn's disguise.
And when the sideshow barker beckons,
I'll take a step inside.

Bart Edelman's poetry collections include *Crossing the Hackensack* (Prometheus Press), *Under Damaris' Dress* (Lightning Publications), *The Alphabet of Love* (Red Hen Press), *The Gentle Man* (Red Hen Press), *The Last Mojito* (Red Hen Press), *The Geographer's Wife* (Red Hen Press), and *Whistling to Trick the Wind* (Meadowlark Press). He has taught at Glendale College, where he edited *Eclipse*, a literary journal, and, most recently, in the MFA program at Antioch University, Los Angeles. His work has been widely anthologized in textbooks. He lives in Pasadena, California.

Life After

Karla Linn Merrifield

He'll never know a change has come over me. I can't show him the latest little heartache, latest minor disappointment. He's beyond lines badly broken. Dead poets pass no pipe, dead poets hear no word. So he no longer reads how I've written of him posthumously in lisping poems to mourn the disintegrated muse. Imperfectly garner again a few particular molecules of that idiosyncratic Georgia beau.

Etowah River
ceases to flow with old souls.
The paddle is still.

Karla Linn Merrifield has 16 books to her credit. Her newest poetry collection, *My Body the Guitar*, recently nominated for the National Book Award, was inspired by famous guitarists and their guitars and published in December 2021 by Before Your Quiet Eyes Publications Holograph Series (Rochester, NY). She is a frequent contributor to *The Songs of Eretz Poetry Review*. Web site: https://www.karlalinnmerrifield.org/; blog at https://karlalinnmerrifield.wordpress.com/; Tweet @LinnMerrifiel; https://www.facebook.com/karlalinn.merrifield.

Contemplating the Crescent
Tara Menon

The crescent moon is a fuzzy fruit
like the furry peach on my quartz counter.

If I say a mantra for Hanuman,
it will be within my grasp.

It will taste like ambrosia.
The memory forever tingling
on my tongue and mouth.

The earth will be dark for an eternity.
The studded sky will miss the smile
that lit up our species and soon we will
wither and die.

One person's rapaciousness extinguishing life.
Better the peach within my reach.

Tara Menon is an Indian-American writer based in Lexington, Massachusetts. Her latest fiction has appeared or is forthcoming in *The Hong Kong Review, Litro, The Bookends Review, Rio Grande Review,* and *The Evening Street Review*. Her most recent poems have been published or are forthcoming in *Arlington Literary Journal, Global South, San Pedro River Review, The Loch Raven Review,* and *The Tiger Moth Review*. She is also a book reviewer and essayist whose pieces have appeared in many journals.

Now That Hay Fever Season Has Passed
D.C. Buschmann

I like to feel the heat
        bear down on my face
in late fall
        as the breeze cools and gentles my arms
while I walk a mile or two
        with my neighbor.

I like to roll my tongue
        over a Tootsie Roll,
smash
        it with my teeth,
taste the burst of satisfaction
        while I read.

I like the soothing view on my patio
        of vincas and marigolds
nourished by rainwater
        collected
in the big blue bowl
        bought years ago.

I don't like mind-jolting racket
        made by
lawnmowers,
        edging equipment,
tree extractors,
        or root grinders.

I prefer to sit in my wicker chair,
        absorb nature's notes and tones,
watch two senior dogs chase squirrels
        and decipher canine codes
in the grass
        while I attempt to simply *take a moment*.

D.C. Buschmann is a retired editor and reading specialist. Her poem, "Death Comes for a Friend," was the Editor's Choice in *Poetry Quarterly*, Winter 2018. Her work has been published in many journals including Kurt Vonnegut Museum and Library's *So it Goes Literary Journal, The Adirondack Review, Tipton Poetry Journal,* and *Red Coyote*. She lives in Carmel, Indiana with husband Nick and miniature schnauzers Cupcake and Coco. Her first poetry collection, *Nature: Human and Otherwise*, was published in February 2021.

Writer's Block
R L Swihart

I didn't write a poem for over a week

A close friend died. Someone I only knew from a distance
died, but he temporarily resurrected two beautiful
souls

I flew here and drove there, always listening
to the subtle rhythms of the engine

I waited for the sun to come out. I waited for the rain
to stop

Instead of writing a poem I wrote condolences

I wrote a note to a shut-in about the parade

I booked a room near Shelter Valley and scribbled
plans about my visit

I rolled out of bed (but it was your alarm). Showered first.
Left imprints on two eyelids refusing
to wake

R L Swihart was born in Michigan but now resides in Long Beach California. His work has sparsely dotted both the Net and hardcopy literary journals (*Cordite, Pif Magazine, The Literary Bohemian, Offcourse, Otoliths, Denver Quarterly, Quadrant Magazine, The Bookends Review*). His third book of poetry was released July 2020: *Woodhenge*.

Self Portrait as a Record Needle

Sophia Upshaw

I come home from work,
a red pail overflowing with words, eager
to make sandcastles out of sentences.
I unclasp my bra & toss it on the armchair,
eat my black bean burger with a fork & knife,
and set tea lights ablaze. I place my gilded
Goodwill candelabra on the window sill,
a reverse SOS signal to show the world,
or at least the dog walkers, that tonight,
I'm more than okay, that all that's missing
is a bubble bath – the aroma of lavender
stems tied to sandalwood softening
my shoulder blades, Chet Baker spinning
in vinyl circles. He pins his love to his lapel
and I soften, melting over my desk
like warm butter. I am as dainty as a record
needle, a Two Buck Chuck sommelier,
sipping Pinot Noir from a mason jar.
All I need is an audience, a darling little
crow to knock at my window with his beak,
candle flames dancing across beady black eyes –
I'll read him this poem and turn his feathers pink,
orange, blue – the color of the sunset
as it thaws across the sky, a celestial billboard
advertising an evening well spent.

Sophia Upshaw lives in Tallahassee, Florida. Her work has been featured in *The Kudzu Review* and *Mistake House Magazine*.

the flood
Janelle Finamore

The unhinged deck floating, it's head
Barely above water
Already rotten

The tapestry of my swinging emotions washed onto marshy shore
Waterlogged

I can't even salvage your love

Your tears twist into a figure eight
Snip snip

Unknot me
Unfettered, liberated as

Your face skates gently towards me,
power, purpose
of a hungry sea lion

A moat grows around my heart.
Please sift through this mess and find
Heavy oars

Row to me

Janelle Finamore is a musician, poet, and teacher located in Orange County, California. Most recently, her work appeared in *Sad Girls Lit*, *Tipton Poetry Journal*, *Poet Magazine*, *Humans of the World*, *A Thin Slice of Anxiety*, *Arlijo*, *Literary Heist*, *Route 7*, *Academy of the Heart&Mind*, *Ariel Chart*, *Literary Yard*, *Spillwords*, and others. Janelle was Poet of the Month for Moon Tide Press and her fairy tale "The Girl Who Stuck Out Like a Sore Thumb" was published in *Bohemia magazine*. She is also an active member of various poetry workshops. Her chapbook *The Power of Silly Putty and Lipstick Kisses* is available on Amazon. Janelle has featured her book in poetry venues in California including The Ugly Mug and others.

Almost Winter
Bruce Levine

The air cools to an almost chill
As the remnants of fall leaves
Blow across the landscape

Early morning frost on windshields
Mark the days moving forward
As the calendar ticks toward the
   winter solstice

Shortening days and longer nights
Reflecting on the senses
In a multitude of feelings

Winter on the horizon
In the shadows of the day
As the grayness of sunsets
   forecasts the change

At the end of the year
And the harbinger of springtime
Almost winter leads to the next rebirth

Bruce Levine has spent his life as a writer of fiction and poetry and as a music and theatre professional. A 2019 *Pushcart Prize* Poetry nominee, a 2021 *Spillwords Press Awards* winner, the *Featured Writer* in WestWard Quarterly Summer 2021 and his bio is featured in "*Who's Who of Emerging Writers 2020.*" Bruce has over three hundred works published on over twenty-five on-line journals including *Ariel Chart, Spillwords, The Drabble*; in over seventy print books including *Poetry Quarterly, Haiku Journal, Tipton Poetry Journal; Halcyon Days Founder's Favourites* (on-line and print) and his shows have been produced in New York and around the country. His work is dedicated to the loving memory of his late wife, Lydia Franklin. A native Manhattanite, Bruce now lives and writes in Maine. Visit him at www.brucelevine.com

The Now of Now
Paul Lojeski

Between mass shootings
Trees continue to mind
Their own business,
While the rest of us
Prepare for the worst.

No Jet Lag
Paul Lojeski

Sixty-thousand miles an hour speeding around
The sun. One-thousand miles an hour spinning
On its axis. Yet I walk to the mailbox, as if the
Ground beneath me isn't moving at all. If that
Isn't a miracle, then I don't know what is.

Paul Lojeski was born and raised in Lakewood, Ohio. He attended Oberlin College. His poetry has appeared online and in print. He lives in Port Jefferson, New York.

Before Social Media
Arvilla Fee

Before people showed pictures of their
sandwiches, before you had to reveal every
thought and feeling, before the meme wars,
before all that misinformation (according to
those who make such judgments), before
adding friends you never knew, before cats
talked and goats wore tutus, before you knew
Susan was pregnant before her husband did,
before you knew tweets didn't come from
birds, before you snap-insta-chatted-grammed
every five minutes, before your phone sprouted
like a tree branch out of your palm, before
headlines were click-bait (and quite untrue),
before you compared your life to Karen's—with
her house and polished children and three-car
garage, before you blocked people with one
click—you happily ate bologna, watched TV
only when men landed on the moon, minded
your own, fed your non-talking cat, had no idea
Susan was pregnant until she was eight-months
along and you ran into her at the grocery store,
birds tweeted in the trees, you snapped beans
and talked over the backyard fence, clutched a
toddler in each hand (completely unpolished),
didn't know a single person named Karen, and
blocked people with the solid slam of your front door.

Arvilla Fee teahes English Composition for Clark State College in Ohio, and is the poetry editor for the *San Antonio Review*. She has been published in numerous presses including *Poetry Quarterly, Inwood Indiana, 50 Haikus, Contemporary Haibun Online, Drifting Sands Haibun, Teach Write, Acorn, Stone Poetry Quarterly, Bright Flash Literary Review, San Antonio Review* & others. She won the Rebecca Lard Award for best poem in the Spring 2020 issue of *Poetry Quarterly*. Her poetry book, *The Human Side*, comes out in 2023.

The Stars As They Die
George Freek

In the distance the clouds
pay me no mind. They exist
in otherworldly time.
They dissolve into night.
The stars appear dismembered.
They barely shed light.
I can see nothing,
nothing but the shadow
of a make-believe blackbird,
in the shadow
of a make-believe tree,
and the moon
lowers her eyes,
when she gazes at me.

George Freek is a poet/playwright living in Belvidere, Illionois. George Freek's poetry appears in numerous Journals and Reviews. His poem "Written At Blue Lake" was recently nominated for a Pushcart Prize. His poem "Enigmatic Variations" was also recently nominated for Best of the Net. His collection *Melancholia* is published by Red Wolf Editions.

Thinning of the Veil
Michelle Hartman

A chill breeze brings whispers of crows.
    Natter and mumble
as they leave items   for brewing spells.
The stag and tower cards have dominated
    my readings this morning.   So damp the day
the sage almost refused to light.
Autumn sits at my table,   staring at the fire
she grows shorter, more guant   less respected each year.
It is not what you look at   but what you see,
    she sees the world burning. Her leaves
  cannot fall from dead trees.
We wait, she and I   for the thinning of the veil.
Our sisters around the world prepare. It went wrong
when we taught our children   to fear witches
not those who burned them. When we leave
    we will take hope with us.

I can write you a world
Michelle Hartman

Talk sense to a fool and he calls you foolish ~ Euripides

I do not write   what I see in your world
I write what I see   in mine.
The cliche is that writers   are introverts, not true.
We have a fantastic reality,   made by us for us
    wish not to spend time   in this melting slag heap
you think is still a viable abode.
There is time before lunch   to sit on the telephone lines
read the morning paper.   A great place to catch up
on crow gossip,   the latest news of the Fey.
A skeleton has come to my door,
he is peddling mirrors   and clothespins.
I think I can get him   to stay for tea.
Maybe he'll have something
     to fix the frost on the carpet.

Michelle Hartman's fourth book, *Wanton Disarray*, along with her other books, *Disenchanted and Disgruntled, Irony and Irreverence*, and *The Lost Journal of my Second Trip to Purgatory*, are available on Amazon and Barnes & Noble. Hartman's work has appeared in over three hundred publications. She lives in Fort Worth, Texas, and is the former editor of *Red River Review*. She recently won the John and Miriam Morris Memorial Chapbook contest, sponsored by the Alabama State Poetry Society. Hartman holds a BS in Political Science-Pre Law from Texas Wesleyan University and a Certificate in Paralegal Studies from Tarrant County Community College. She was recently named Distinguished Alumni by TCC.

Most Poems
Michael Lee Johnson

Most poems are pounded out
in emotional flesh, sometimes
physical skin scalped feelings.
It's a Jesus hanging on a cross
a Mary kneeling at the bottom
not knotted in love but roped,
a blade of a bowie knife
heavenward.
I look for the kicker line
the close at the bottom
seek a public poetry forum
to cheer my aspirations on.
I hear those far away voices
carrying my life away —
a retreat into insanity.

Michael Lee Johnson is an internationally published poet in 44 countries, has several published poetry books, has been nominated for 4 Pushcart Prize awards and 6 Best of the Net nominations, and has over 266 poetry videos on YouTube.

5.1 cm

Cameron Morse

Diameter the length of
the middle knuckle of my index finder
in right frontal lobe, falling
short of golf ball tumor, the standard
comparison for hail so big we bring one
to the freezer as a keepsake,
a for the sake of. I never measured it out
by the light of my iPhone before

this growth is putting me out of business.
My whole left arm is a power
outage. Outrage consumes the tenements
of my body. Pressed against a wall
swiveling down the sewer drain
what are they these cells that build
precariously? What crawled out of the swamp?
The same primordial sea spawned
you and me, our machine life.

Cameron Morse is Senior Reviews editor at *Harbor Review* and the author of eight collections of poetry. His first collection, *Fall Risk*, won Glass Lyre Press's 2018 Best Book Award. His book of unrhymed sonnets, *Sonnetizer*, is forthcoming from Kelsay Books. He holds an MFA from the University of Kansas City-Missouri and lives in Independence, Missouri, with his wife Lili and three children. For more information, check out his Facebook page or website.

The Wrong Place
Tawn Parent

"I don't think we're in the right place,"
my son said,
looking up at the sign above the desk.
"What's oncology?" he asked.
It was my turn to look up at Eli,
(my tall manboy with the baby face),
into those wondering hazel eyes.
My tongue curled around the word,
reluctant to release its awful power.
Big breath.
"It means cancer," I said.

My husband came in from the parking lot
and we three trooped down a hall,
into a small room,
without enough space to breathe,
sat in hard plastic chairs,
and heard from an unsmiling doctor,
aggressive, unusual,
large tumor, sarcoma,
blood in the belly,
more detailed pathology,
bone marrow biopsy,
bone scan, body scan,
port-o-cath, clinical trials,
chemotherapy, radiation,
nausea, vomiting, losing hair,
treatment before Christmas,
no more school this year.

"No school!" Eli exclaimed,
as if that were the worst of the news.
But perhaps it was the only bit he could grasp
in the soup of this surreal conversation.
We sat and stared,
dry-eyed and numb,
nodded, signed, took appointment cards
into helpless hands,
and slowly rose.
Our legs somehow carried us
from the small room,
back down the hall
and out of that right and wrong place
into the gray afternoon.

A native of Indianapolis, **Tawn Parent** has been a professional writer and editor for 30 years. She has worked primarily for business publications and also served as proofreader for two books. She holds a B.A. in journalism and French from Indiana University and a master's degree in English language acquisition from Marian University. She is working on a compilation of poems about her young son's cancer journey.

The god you are given
Mark Vogel

When I awake I shall behold my face in righteousness;
I shall be satisfied with beholding thy form. ~ Rewritten Psalm 17

Hearing quiet commands coming from out and in,
immersed in the breathing like a dog fat with smells,
no longer in the dream, but autonomous,
stuffed with free will floating in diaphanous light,
welcoming the persistent newly crafted story,
eyes open, the day colored with shifting window movement
as if smiling for a god with dimensions I can handle,
the presence arranging the in and out—
peace content in this now—
even knowing off the ridge partier pigs snort,
their rations smeared on snouts as the light
shifts and the shadows appear.
For the god of habit whispers (again)
and new boundaries appear—a sentient turtle
crawls like a slow meditation in the maturing sun
as I rise to ablutions and breakfast, jewelweed
and buttercups, all manner of explosive yellow red green.
This god says: *prune it, and it will grow,*
then rewrites again and again the one psalm so it fits.
Sometimes legs fold together, waiting for
the gesture that designates the correct path.
Forgotten, the realm of sleep that glued tight parallel stories.
In this immediacy more felt than understood,
clouds swirl and light builds, and today's gentle
blowing message travels from miles away.
The delight in moving, aware, is enough.

Mark Vogel lives at the back of a Blue Ridge holler with his wife, Susan Weinberg, an accomplished fiction and creative non-fiction writer, and two foster sons. He currently is an Emeritus Professor of English at Appalachian State University in Boone, North Carolina. Poems and short stories have appeared in several dozen literary journals.

Barney Fife Finds Sweet Revenge

Eugene Stevenson

Consider then the tough-guy Barney Fife,
chafing second fiddle to Andy Taylor, always
a deputy, object of derisive laughter even
in the face of, *Now I'm being serious here.*

His troubles begin when he begins to think,
compound as he kicks through his thoughts,
manifest as he avers to be what he is not,
People are going to respect me after this.

He has had to wait decades for his opportunity:
black sunglasses, black equipment belt,
black Kevlar vest, black Glock in the holster,
black telescoping baton. *Fear on the hoof.*

Barney grows a swagger, hours in the gym,
practices a *Drop Dead* scowl in the mirror,
screams commands in the shower, falls in
love with his ICE uniform. *Sweet revenge.*

Eugene Stevenson , son of immigrants, father of expatriates, lives in the Smoky Mountains of North Carolina. Eisenhower Fellow, Pushcart Prize nominee & author of *The Population of Dreams* (Finishing Line Press 2022), his poems have appeared in *The Galway Review, The Hudson Review, San Pedro River Review, Third Wednesday, Tipton Poetry Journal* & *Washington Square Review* among others.

The Autistic Boy and the Hose
John Grey

He loved having the hose turned on him,
that stream of cool liquid
splashing every part of his body.
It didn't even have to be a hot day.

He would reach up
and try to catch to catch the water
but it would slip through his fingers
or slap against his palms
and splatter in all directions.

He connected to that flow
more than he did with people.
Towel him dry and he'd be friendless.

Sid's Future
John Grey

What do you want to be when you grow up?
she asked the class.

Lots of doctors and lawyers.
But only the one who volunteered —
I'm gonna sell knockoff hand-bags like my old man.

The girls spoke up with perfect pitch,
The boys erupted, but gently, like bubbles on a surface.

I wanna be bugged by the cops, he continued.
    Where's your vendor's license?
    Did this stuff fall off the back of the truck?

The others were rehearsed by the homes they came from.
He was engineered by visits to the big house.

John Grey is an Australian poet, US resident now living in Rhode Island, recently published in *Sheepshead Review, Stand, Washington Square Review* and *Floyd County Moonshine*. Latest books, *Covert, Memory Outside The Head*, and *Guest Of Myself* are available through Amazon. Work upcoming in the *McNeese Review, Rathalla Review* and *Open Ceilings*.

Dogs May Smell God
Bruce Campbell

I think dogs meditate – when you see them lying quiet,
alert and attentive to every breeze, every sound –
I'd add, if I could, the cast of light, but that's more in *our* diet –
to every sense, anyway, that they're best evolved to use –
attending to what's concrete, most in this moment.
And I think that's where God's still big news,
right on the edge of this here right now –
if anywhere, here the Tao's most touchable.
If there were and could be no other bestowment,
what better than a heartfelt sense of "Wow!"?
If God infuses everything, here's where the infusion bubbles –
where creation happens, where new is found.

I think dogs may smell God –
that being their primary sense, it stands to reason,
though it will shock some that I say so
and seem to others only odd.
I say this 'cause my dog seems more at peace than,
on my best days, I do.
And I say this because God's there to be seen
if not by us much smelt.
I say this because I'm keen to know,
if unsure the way to pursue,
whatever it is my dog's just felt
and where, while lying still, she's been.

[This poem was first published in the Summer 2021 issue of *The Missouri Review*]

Bruce Campbell

This is how I see us:
God below, human above –
spider above, rhino above.
Fly, antelope, polar bear, trout, tiger, mantis, lemur,
platypus, pterodactyl, trilobite, mosasaur,
albatross also above.
Individual consciousnesses down so far.
Below that, tapping into – being, actually –
unavoidably and irrevocably, irreversibly and unrefutably,
the one consciousness we all are basically.
Separate, singular, private, and seemingly complete,
but only so so far.

And permeable.

[This poem was first published in the Summer 2021 issue of *The Missouri Review*]

Bruce Campbell is, by day, Scientific Editor at the Magee-Women's Research Institute at the University of Pittsburgh. In the evenings, he is a sometimes composer of microtonal music.

Importance

Ken Poyner

A woman has climbed over
The rickety fire escape outside
A building's sixth floor window.

People begin to gather at the base
Of the building. It is assumed
She has some connection to the sixth floor

Window. Perhaps it leads to
An apartment. Perhaps it is an office
Where she works, clerical or cleaning,

Or with numbers. Her heels
On the ledge of the fire escape platform,
She reaches back to the rail,

Cupping it underhand and leaning
In a series of acute angles forward.
Below, the debate is will she fall

Or jump, or will someone at the window
Step out to gather her heroically by the waist.
A woman with her pre-teen son

Collects at the back of the still growing
Crowd. She draws her hand over
Her son's eyes, as the woman is naked.

Ken Poyner lives in Norfolk, Virginia. This year he has published several pieces of microfiction and between twenty and thirty poems, three of which have been nominated for a Pushcart Prize.

In the voices of birds
Nancy Huxtable Mohr

he dresses for breakfast and our walk
spills egg on his clean shirt
more buttons again   forward through
the black now with white cane
      tapping   tapping   tapping
outside he holds tight on my arm
two steps behind me   we listen
for the familiar romance
      in the voices of birds
stop, surrender our breath in imitation
edges of our bodies vanish
      and no further sorrow possible
in any form.

Nancy Huxtable Mohr is a retired teacher. Her work explores motherhood, embodiment, the climate crisis, and nature. She lives part-time in Northern California and Upstate New York. She considers herself a farm girl although it's been a long time since she milked a cow. Her work can be found in many journals, most recently in *Cider Press Review, BeZine, Concho River Review, Avocet, Rogue Agent*, and others. More of her work can be found on her website at www.nancyhuxtablemohr.org and Instagram @nancy.mohr

Boatman

Haro Lee

You are passed down the riverbed
passed in fist and foot
in belly and arse
in unkissed scalp.

All day your breaths tip you from
side to side, letting a little water
into your boat, bursting
a little dam between her legs.

And then, the canal splits in blood and water
and they can see your crown.
Welcome, love,
to your first resurrection.

Your lips take her milk and she notices
how the ends of your hair
hold pohutukawa in full bloom.
Bees carry their honey towards you.

Haro Lee is a Korean poet who teaches English in South Korea. Her work has been published and is forthcoming in *Michigan Quarterly Review, Zone 3 Press, The Offing, The Indianapolis Review, The Texas Review, Anhinga Press, RHINO Poetry, Dryland Lit,* and *Ghost City Press,* among others. She was also the recipient of *Epiphany Magazine's* Breakout 8 Writers Prize.

At Lewis and Clark Landing

Katherine Hoerth

Another perfect April afternoon
along the river: spring is in full bloom,
the marigolds show off their amber hues
in flowerboxes, patches of fresh-laid sod
shimmer with an embarrassment of green.
Young catalpas planted in a row
along the loamy shoreline settle in—ideal
for their shallow roots and fragrant flowers.

A toddler races to the brand-new sandbox
with a shovel in her hand. She'll dig
perhaps to China, fill her pail with earth.
A swing set moans as someone breaks it in.
The jungle gym, with wet paint, sits untouched.

The Missouri river lazes on
through the season as it has for eons,
before it had this name, before it carved
this landing place of history and lead.
Beneath the thin veneer of peace, what lies?
A foot of clay, a superfund, the bones
of the past. We've covered up such darkness here.
We pray our children never dig too deep.

Katherine Hoerth is the author of five poetry collections, including the *forthcoming Flare Stacks in Full Bloom* (Texas Review Press, 2021). She is an assistant professor at Lamar University and editor of Lamar University Literary Press. Her writing interests include eco-poetry, feminism, and formalism. She is a member of the Texas Institute of Letters and lives near Houston.

Mercy

Lynette Lamp

1.
My husband drew the line at killing
a baby mole. But those tunnels in the yard
came from somewhere. He drove the mole
to the woods, left it there. Crueler than any
shovel, but he wasn't the one
doing the killing. Like Pontius Pilate,
he washed his hands of it.

2.
Something had been nesting inside
our daughter's outgrown dirt-bike boots,
slumped in a dark corner—insides full
of paper scraps and dry pasta. The home
was abandoned home when I found it,
but I would have dumped the contents
even if something were nestled inside.

3.
Our child carefully trapped a spider
in her room, freed it outside. She knew
it was there for weeks, willing to share her space
until it bit her on the ankle. I've sanctioned
death for less: shit on my deck,
bird body-slams on my windows.
But while weeding my gardens yesterday,
I tiptoed around a sleeping fawn,
even though its mother ate my roses.

Lynette Lamp is a practicing family physician and recent graduate of the Spalding University MFA program. She has had previous poems published in *JAMA (Journal of American Medical Association), The Pharos,* and *Annals of Internal Medicine.* Lynette lives in Winona, Minnesota.

The Runner
Alessio Zanelli

On feet of dreams the runner's headed to land's end.
She knows the horizon keeps receding while she's running,
but she runs as though it didn't.
A finish line is not her aim.
Along the pathway time's not measured in seconds but in paces,
in fact a runner's time and space commingle.
The run will come to a stop where dreams dissolve,
and dreams don't hinge on time or space
but on the run itself.
Land's end is but a moving sight, the pathway a circle.

Alessio Zanelli is an Italian poet who writes in English and whose work has appeared in over 200 literary journals from 16 countries. His fifth original collection, titled *The Secret Of Archery*, was published in 2019 by Greenwich Exchange Publishing (London). For more information please visit www.alessiozanelli.it.

Less

Kit Kennedy

Flora divides her day into three equal segments:
into the sun into the fire into the tiger's eye
offering no clue why manual typewriters hold such interest

nor when Flora sees a fried egg poppy, why
that evening she dreams of ink
nor why Flora worries when the apple falls, who will catch?

the door opens, the door closes upon interior weather
all boxes accounted for, labeled, sealed
soon the door opens again only to shut permanently

Kit Kennedy is a queer elder living in Walnut Creek, California. She has published 7 collections including "while eating oysters" (CLWN WR BKS, Brooklyn, NY). Work has appeared in *Tipton Poetry Journal, Great Weather for Media, First Literary Review-East, Gyroscope, Glass*, Muse Pie Press, among others. She serves as Poet in Residence of SF Bay Times and Resident Poet at Ebenezer Lutheran "herchurch." Please visit: http://poetrybites.blogspot.com.

Out of Reach, Out of Touch
Tia Paul-Louis

From a clavier harmonizing
Chopin and Schubert
I rose –

lifted like a beam in the sky
till the outrageous waves of the Pacific
swallowed me and silence
became a wobbly gaze.

I've not heard anything for days.

I can't tell if I'm sitting
or lying down as I become less sober,
yet, more conscious, with my lips
pressed against a shadow with no form:
a shadow I sense will never leave me

like the others did.
The others. The beings
I'm afraid to call human. The ones
who vowed rescue but set traps and fire.
They won't come anymore.

Born in the Caribbean and raised in the U.S., **Tia Paul-Louis** began writing songs at age 11, then experimented with poetry during high school. She earned a BA in English/Creative Writing from the University of South Florida along with a M.F.A in Creative Writing from National University in California. Her works have appeared in literary magazines such as *The Voices Project, Ethos Literary Journal,* and *Rabbit Catastrophe Review.* Some of her favorite authors and poets include Langston Hughes, Emily Dickinson, Maya Angelou and Edgar Allan Poe. Apart from writing, Paul-Louis enjoys music, photography, acting and cooking, though she mostly finds herself and others through poetry.

Curl

Ruth Holzer

The lock of light brown hair
that he kept in his wallet,
pressed in tissue paper,
that he'd look at now and then
with renewed pleasure, my curl
of silken newborn hair,
I placed beneath his folded hands,
one thing he could take with him, after all.

Ruth Holzer lives in Virginia and is the author of eight chapbooks, most recently, *Living in Laconia* (Gyroscope Press) and *Among the Missing* (Kelsay Books). Her poems have appeared in *Blue Unicorn, Faultline, Slant, Poet Lore, Connecticut River Review* and *Plainsongs*, among other journals and anthologies. She has received several Pushcart Prize nominations.

Spear-child
Saraswati Nagpal

Before I grew ears, was your voice—
shiver on ectoderm
dawn in amniotic sky
silk in placental
dream
that split

I slithered out, the world a bright fuzz
your cries red with love and
blood I heard

True North, your voice

was starlight
fire, river, sun
fed my bones, your words
grew me, grew
inside me like
fire-seeds, and I became
a forest of thunder,
lightning in my tongue.

Saraswati Nagpal is an Indian writer and poet, a lover of fantasy and sci-fi. Her graphic novels '*Sita, Daughter of the Earth*' and '*Draupadi, the Fire-born Princess*' are retellings of epic Indian myths in the female voice. Her poetry has appeared in *Cathexis Northwest Press* and *The Journal of Radical Wonder*. She is also a classical dancer who choreographs and performs for film and stage. When she isn't writing, she attempts to inspire teenagers by teaching literature. Twitter: @SaraswatiNagpal / Insta: @saraswatinagpal

Fall

Brandon Hansen

despite harvest moon
today the sun's gone postal.
you burn and catch red leaves,
and I'm reminded that falling
is an occasion
for grace.

Brandon Hansen is from a village in northern Wisconsin. He studied writing along Lake Superior, and then trekked out to the mountains, where he earned his MFA as a Truman Capote scholar at the University of Montana. His work has been Pushcart Nominated, and can be found in *The Baltimore Review, Quarterly West, Puerto Del Sol*, and elsewhere. Find him on Twitter: @BatBrandon_

Editor

Barry Harris is editor of the *Tipton Poetry Journal* and four anthologies by Brick Street Poetry: *Mapping the Muse: A Bicentennial Look at Indiana Poetry; Words and Other Wild Things* and *Cowboys & Cocktails:Poems from the True Grit Saloon*, and *Reflections on Little Eagle Creek*. He has published one poetry collection, *Something At The Center*.

Married and father of two grown sons,
Barry lives in Brownsburg, Indiana and is retired from Eli Lilly and Company.

His poetry has appeared in *Kentucky Review, Valparaiso Poetry Review, Grey Sparrow, Silk Road Review, Saint Ann's Review, North Dakota Quarterly, Boston Literary Magazine, Night Train, Silver Birch Press, Flying Island, Awaken Consciousness, Writers' Bloc, Red-Headed Stepchild* and *Laureate: The Literary Journal of Arts for Lawrence*. One of his poems was on display at the National Museum of Sport and another is painted on a barn in Boone County, Indiana as part of Brick Street Poetry's Word Hunger public art project. His poems are also included in these anthologies: *From the Edge of the Prairie; Motif 3: All the Livelong Day;* and *Twin Muses: Art and Poetry*.

He graduated a long time ago with a major in English from Ball State University.

Review: *Ticker* by Mark Neely

Reviewed by Barry Harris

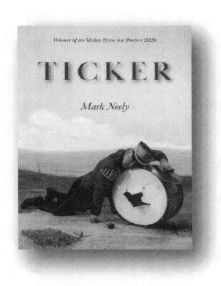

Title: Ticker

Author: Mark Neely

Year: 2021

Publisher: Lost Horse Press

Ticker is a unique book of poems centered around a central character, Bruce. *Ticker* was the winner of the Idaho Prize for Poetry in 2020. Each poem is either about Bruce, about things happening to or centered around Bruce's life, or what Bruce is doing or thinking when events occur in the world we share with Bruce.

So who is Bruce and just what is ticking?

In "The Economy Stupid," Bruce is:

> Like a Taco Bell built
> on the site of a desecrated
> burial mound,
>
> . . . it's so easy
>
> being Bruce.
> He's open late.
> He lets anybody in.

Most poems in the book are third person observational poems. There are also several poems, either in the first person, where Bruce takes jittery control of the narrative, or second person, where some essential part of Bruce seems to be urging poor Bruce to awake. These inner dialogue poems all include the word *Subvocal* in the title. The dictionary defines subvocal as an "unarticulated level of speech, comparable to thought."

These subvocal poems delve more deeply into Bruce's inner thoughts. For example, the first poem in the book is titled "Subvocal (Challenger)":

The poem opens with references to a specific period of time. For those too young to remember January 28, 1986 (the day the Space Shuttle Challenger broke apart killing all seven crew members) Neely paints a picture of what else was going on in or around this time:

> Age of *Achille Lauro* and *Rainbow Warrior*,
> of *Mad Max* and the doddering gipper,
>
> of plaid-clad women and mustachioed men
> tossing villains through plate glass. Of Jan Hammer,
>
> *Desperately Seeking Susan*, "Easy Lover,"
> of Gorbachev with his skull cracked open.
>
> Age of Sweetness and the Refrigerator.
> Age of *I love it when a plan comes together*.

To save readers from googling any of these references you might have either long ago forgotten or not yet stumbled across, here is a quick synopsis. The *Achille Lauro* was an Italian ocean liner hijacked off the coast of Egypt by the Palestine Liberation Front. The *Rainbow Warrior* was the flagship of the Greenpeace fleet bombed and sunk by French intelligence agents. *Mad Max* was a series of Australian dystopian action films. The doddering gipper was Ronald Reagan. Jan Hammer wrote the theme song for the 1980s tv show *Miami Vice*. *Desperately Seeking Susan* was Madonna's first major movie. Mikhail Gorbachev was the last leader of the Soviet Union. Sweetness and the Refrigerator were Chicago Bears players Walter Payton and William "The Refrigerator" Perry. Hannibal Smith's catchphrase on the tv show *A-Team* was "I love it when a plan comes together."

So all this had been going on when Bruce tells us this:

> And the jittery schoolroom television where I watched
> the launch become a strange white praying
>
> mantis in the sky. *Obviously a major malfunction...*
>
> Who could have imagined
> all the stupid years to come, the wreckage
>
> falling toward the ocean —
> surface of the suffocating dark.

"Subvocal (Challenger)" opens the book with a bang, introducing us to the life and thoughts of a teenage Bruce facing all the stupid years to come. Beginning with the poem "Oof," we begin to learn some gauzy details of Bruce's life. He is married to Annie. He appears to have an unnamed ex-wife; Bruce and Annie have lost an unborn child and later have other children, although only Bruce Jr. is named explicitly. There is a hint of a daughter ("Soon yr own / daughter will be hooted at by terrible / sad men").

"Oof" is about getting older:

> A flurry of marriages, births. Then pause —
> the generation
> wringing itself out. Welcome to the long
> trough of middle age, where our hero flinches
>
> as he bends to tie his shoe.
> Annie says you know you're getting old
> if you pull yourself from the car
> with an involuntary *oof*.
>
> Bruce makes such noises all the livelong day,
> an orchestra of grunts and rumbles
> led by a sadist with a bent baton.

Now that you have read that last stanza, feel free to glance back at the cover photo for an apt visual. The poem ends when Bruce is in a grocery checkout line gazing a few seconds too long at the young "tattooed, crimson-lipped checker."

> *Have a nice day*, she says, then catches
> his delinquent glance and adds a cruel, *Sir,*
> and a pitiless smirk. Poor Bruce,
>
> he isn't sure what happened.
> Gone from suitor to lecher in a wink.
> And really, he's no dirtier than before.

In "Unborn Elegy," we learn about Bruce and Annie's unborn son.

> . . . It's strange
> how Bruce misses him
> this boy he's never met
>
> except as a kick
> in Annie's belly, this
> biohazard bag thrown
>
> out with the bloody
> needles this notion falling
> through him like a stone.

Bruce seems to both love and need Annie. In "Two by Two" we learn that

> Bruce doesn't have much to say
> about Annie. He forgets he's lucky.
> Forgets she's smarter, works
> harder, makes less money . . .
>
> And all the days
> she holds his melancholy
> like a wet, wild animal,
> so he can be happy.

It is tempting to see Bruce as a symbolic Everyman. But an Everyman roiled from decades of struggling like a modern Sisyphus against an unforgiving, unrelenting system. Yet, Bruce appears to want to have faith, to believe.

In "Bruce's Faith," we hear that:

> The secret is to be looking forward
> to something beyond Friday night —
> the Sunday long run or sitting
> in a pew to pray away
> two thousand bloody years.

In "Intelligent Design," Bruce entertains this fantasy:

> He thinks he made the universe
> somehow — scattered stars,
> decided if the trees
> would leaf or needle,
> dressed the beetle
> in medieval armor.
>
> It's not out of the question.
> After he bruned a moon-sized hole
> in the ozone, razed the Amazon,
> turned the endless plains
> into a pile of bison skulls.
>
> It took seven days.
> It took seven billion years.

If Bruce is an Everyman, the image conjured in "Totem" seems to cleverly suggest this.

> Bruce takes
> a swig then
> passes the bottle
>
> to the Bruce
> below and then
> again . . .
>
> Bruce thinks
>
> he'll find the
> real Bruce down
> there, the brave
>
> big-hearted Bruce
> who will lead the rest
> of them to victory. . .
>
> but Bruce knows it's
> no use. There
>
> are nothing but desparate Bruces
> all the way down.

Bruce gives himself a pep talk in "Subvocal (Jefferson Airplane)" within a poem set at Woodstock with a Grace Slick soundtrack.

> Let's get going Bruce! Let's get
> Catullan, Cassanovian, Kenndy-esque.
>
> Make those fuckers wish
> they still had bodies. It's time
>
> to blow this awful subcommittee and take
> a few more dizzy spins around the sun
>
> before yr staring through six feet of Illinois,
> an inch of cake makeup on yr face.
>
> Are you listening? Bruce,
> are you awake?

Now that you are acquainted Bruce, you might be curious about the book title, *Ticker*. There are hints. One hint is the symbolism of a ticker tape parade, suggested by "View From the Highwire":

> Saga in ticker tape
> with no occasion
> for parading, Bruce's
>
> stock is taking
> a dive, his shares
> brought low. . .
>
> The crowd prefers
> a dive, Bruce swanning

> toward the side-
> walk in the tortured
> pose of a body just
> before it becomes
>
> a corpse. . . All that's left
>
> is the idiot mayor
> processing down
> Fourth Avenue
>
> below the jingoistic
> clouds as strips of paper
> spiral in the breeze. . .
>
> wrapping Bruce's
> body so he can
> be born again.

But the smart money is on the heart as a beating force. Bruce's heart. He tells us himself in "Subvocal (Life Support)":

> Hook me up to everything you've got,
> . . . Sew in pig valves, spry and spongy,
>
> a pair of stout bull's balls
> if that's the way it has to be.
>
> . . . as long as sunlight rattles through the blinds
> to shine
>
> on Annie, fierce behind a veil of dust,
> you keep that pig heart pumping in my chest.

And again in "Subvocal (Ticker)" we detect the constant pulse of a beating heart, or is it the beeping of a hospital monitor or a grocery scanner.

> Bleep bleep Bruce. Bleep bleep
> the cornflakes in the scanner beam.
>
> Bleep bleep the birds,
> the 6:00 a.m. alarm. Bleep bleep
>
> the words you think but never say.
> Wake up! It's garbage day . . .
>
> It's time to bleep!
> Time to get to work.

Mark Neely has written a tight, blunt, humorous and sad picture of Bruce and what Bruce represents — perhaps a world increasingly running us down as we strive to find meaning in lives beset by the ticking monotony of an empty culture built on consumerism and mendacity.

Mark Neely is the author of *Beasts of the Hill* and *Dirty Bomb,* both from Oberlin College Press. His third book, *Ticker,* won the Idaho Prize for Poetry and was published by Lost Horse Press in 2021. His awards include an NEA Poetry Fellowship, an Indiana Individual Artist grant, the FIELD Poetry Prize, and the Concrete Wolf Press chapbook award for Four of a Kind. He is a professor of English at Ball State University and a senior editor at *River Teeth: a Journal of Nonfiction Narrative.*

Barry Harris is editor of the *Tipton Poetry Journal* and four anthologies by Brick Street Poetry. He has published one poetry collection, *Something At The Center.*

Married and father of two grown sons, Barry lives in Brownsburg, Indiana and is retired from Eli Lilly and Company.

His poetry has appeared in *Kentucky Review, Valparaiso Poetry Review, Grey Sparrow, Silk Road Review, Saint Ann's Review, North Dakota Quarterly, Boston Literary Magazine, Night Train, Silver Birch Press, Flying Island, Awaken Consciousness, Writers' Bloc, Red-Headed Stepchild* and *Laureate: The Literary Journal of Arts for Lawrence.*

He graduated a long time ago with a major in English from Ball State University.

Contributor Biographies

D.C. Buschmann is a retired editor and reading specialist. Her poem, "Death Comes for a Friend," was the Editor's Choice in *Poetry Quarterly*, Winter 2018. Her work has been published in many journals including Kurt Vonnegut Museum and Library's *So it Goes Literary Journal, The Adirondack Review, Tipton Poetry Journal, and Red Coyote*. She lives in Carmel, Indiana with husband Nick and miniature schnauzers Cupcake and Coco. Her first poetry collection, *Nature: Human and Otherwise*, was published in February 2021.

Bruce Campbell is, by day, Scientific Editor at the Magee-Women's Research Institute at the University of Pittsburgh. In the evenings, he is a sometimes composer of microtonal music.

Dan Carpenter has published poetry and fiction in *Illuminations, Pearl, Poetry East, Southern Indiana Review, Maize, Flying Island, Pith, The Laurel Review, Sycamore Review, Prism International, Fiction, Hopewell Review* and other journals. A collection of columns written for *The Indianapolis Star*, where he earned his living, was published by Indiana University Press in 1993 with the title *Hard Pieces: Dan Carpenter's Indiana*. Dan has published two books of poems, *The Art He'd Sell for Love* (Cherry Grove, 2015) and *More Than I Could See* (Restoration, 2009); and two books of non-fiction.

After 34 years with Eli Lilly and Company, **Brendan Crowley** set up his own consulting and executive coaching business, Brendan Crowley Advisors LLC. He helps executives grow in their roles and careers. Brendan is originally from Ireland and lives with his wife Rosaleen in Zionsville, Indiana. He has a passion for photography and loves taking photographs of his home country, Ireland, and here in Indiana.

A nine time Pushcart nominee in both prose and poetry, **Liz Dolan** has published two poetry collections. Her ten grandchildren pepper her life. Liz lives in Rehobeth Beach, Delaware.

Hollie Dugas lives in New Mexico. Her work has been selected to be included in *Barrow Street, Reed Magazine, Crab Creek Review, Redivider, Porter House Review, Pembroke, Salamander, Poet Lore, Watershed Review, Mud Season Review, Little Patuxent Review, The Louisville Review, The Penn Review, Chiron Review, Louisiana Literature*, and *CALYX*. Most recently, her poem was selected as winner of the 22nd Annual Lois Cranston Memorial Poetry Prize at CALYX, in addition to, the 2022 Heartwood Poetry Prize. Hollie has been a finalist twice for the Peseroff Prize at *Breakwater Review*, Greg Grummer Poetry Prize at *Phoebe*, *Fugue's* Annual Contest, and has received Honorable Mention in *Broad River Review*. Additionally, "A Woman's Confession #5,162" was selected as the winner of *Western Humanities Review* Mountain West Writers' Contest (2017). Recently, Hollie has been nominated for a 2020 Pushcart Prize and for inclusion in Best New Poets 2021. She is currently a member on the editorial board for *Off the Coast*.

Bart Edelman's poetry collections include *Crossing the Hackensack* (Prometheus Press), *Under Damaris' Dress* (Lightning Publications), *The Alphabet of Love* (Red Hen Press), *The Gentle Man* (Red Hen Press), *The Last Mojito* (Red Hen Press), *The Geographer's Wife* (Red Hen Press), and *Whistling to Trick the Wind* (Meadowlark Press). He has taught at Glendale College, where he edited *Eclipse*, a literary journal, and, most recently, in the MFA program at Antioch University, Los Angeles. His work has been widely anthologized in textbooks published by City Lights Books, Etruscan Press, Fountainhead Press, Harcourt Brace, Longman, McGraw-Hill, Prentice Hall, Simon & Schuster, Thomson/Heinle, the University of Iowa Press, Wadsworth, and others. He lives in Pasadena, California.

Arvilla Fee teahes English Composition for Clark State College in Ohio, and is the poetry editor for the *San Antonio Review*. She has been published in numerous presses including *Poetry Quarterly, Inwood Indiana, 50 Haikus, Contemporary Haibun Online, Drifting Sands Haibun, Teach Write, Acorn, Stone Poetry Quarterly, Bright Flash Literary Review, San Antonio Review* & others. She won the Rebecca Lard Award for best poem in the Spring 2020 issue of *Poetry Quarterly*. Her poetry book, *The Human Side*, comes out in 2023.

Janelle Finamore is a musician, poet, and teacher located in Orange County, California. Most recently, her work appeared in *Sad Girls Lit, Tipton Poetry Journal, Poet Magazine, Humans of the World, A Thin Slice of Anxiety, Arlijo, Literary Heist, Route 7, Academy of the Heart&Mind, Ariel Chart, Literary Yard, Spillwords*, and others. Janelle was Poet of the Month for Moon Tide Press and her fairy tale "The Girl Who Stuck Out Like a Sore Thumb" was published in *Bohemia magazine*. She is also an active member of various poetry workshops. Her chapbook *The Power of Silly Putty and Lipstick Kisses* is available on Amazon. Janelle has featured her book in poetry venues in California including The Ugly Mug and others.

Rosemary Freedman is a poet, a painter and an advanced practice nurse. She has 7 children and lives in Noblesville, Indiana with her husband Jack. Rosemary enjoys growing peonies and tending her large garden. She is a graduate of Indiana University. Rosemary is currently working toward her masters of fine arts in poetry at Butler University.

George Freek is a poet/playwright living in Belvidere, Illionois. George Freek's poetry appears in numerous Journals and Reviews. His poem "Written At Blue Lake" was recently nominated for a Pushcart Prize. His poem "Enigmatic Variations" was also recently nominated for Best of the Net. His collection *Melancholia* is published by Red Wolf Editions.

James Green has worked as a naval officer, deputy sheriff, high school English teacher, professor of education, and administrator in both public schools and universities. Recipient of two Fulbright grants, he has served as a visiting scholar at the University of Limerick in Ireland and the National Chung Cheng University in Taiwan. In addition to academic publications, including three books, Green is the author of three chapbooks of poetry and a fourth, *Long Journey Home*, is forthcoming after winning the Charles Dickson Chapbook Contest sponsored by the Georgia Poetry Society., Individual poems have appeared in literary magazines in England, Ireland, and the United States. He resides in Muncie, Indiana.

John Grey is an Australian poet, US resident now living in Rhode Island, recently published in *Sheepshead Review, Stand, Washington Square Review* and *Floyd County*

Moonshine. Latest books, *Covert, Memory Outside The Head,* and *Guest Of Myself* are available through Amazon. Work upcoming in the *McNeese Review, Rathalla Review* and *Open Ceilings.*

Brandon Hansen is from a village in northern Wisconsin. He studied writing along Lake Superior, and then trekked out to the mountains, where he earned his MFA as a Truman Capote scholar at the University of Montana. His work has been Pushcart Nominated, and can be found in *The Baltimore Review, Quarterly West, Puerto Del Sol*, and elsewhere. Find him on Twitter: @BatBrandon_

Michelle Hartman's fourth book, *Wanton Disarray*, along with her other books, *Disenchanted and Disgruntled, Irony and Irreverence*, and *The Lost Journal of my Second Trip to Purgatory*, are available on Amazon and Barnes & Noble. Hartman's work has appeared in over three hundred publications. She lives in Fort Worth, Texas, and is the former editor of *Red River Review.* She recently won the John and Miriam Morris Memorial Chapbook contest, sponsored by the Alabama State Poetry Society. Hartman holds a BS in Political Science-Pre Law from Texas Wesleyan University and a Certificate in Paralegal Studies from Tarrant County Community College. She was recently named Distinguished Alumni by TCC.

Katherine Hoerth is the author of five poetry collections, including the *forthcoming Flare Stacks in Full Bloom* (Texas Review Press, 2021). She is an assistant professor at Lamar University and editor of Lamar University Literary Press. Her writing interests include eco-poetry, feminism, and formalism. She is a member of the Texas Institute of Letters and lives near Houston.

Ruth Holzer lives in Virginia and is the author of eight chapbooks, most recently, *Living in Laconia* (Gyroscope Press) and *Among the Missing* (Kelsay Books). Her poems have appeared in *Blue Unicorn, Faultline, Slant, Poet Lore, Connecticut River Review* and *Plainsongs*, among other journals and anthologies. She has received several Pushcart Prize nominations.

Michael Lee Johnson is an internationally published poet in 44 countries, has several published poetry books, has been nominated for 4 Pushcart Prize awards and 6 Best of the Net nominations, and has over 266 poetry videos on YouTube.

Kit Kennedy is a queer elder living in Walnut Creek, California. She has published 7 collections including "while eating oysters" (CLWN WR BKS, Brooklyn, NY). Work has appeared in *Tipton Poetry Journal, Great Weather for Media, First Literary Review-East, Gyroscope, Glass*, Muse Pie Press, among others. She serves as Poet in Residence of SF Bay Times and Resident Poet at Ebenezer Lutheran "herchurch." Please visit: http://poetrybites.blogspot.com/.

Philip C. Kolin is the distinguished Professor of English Emeritus at the University of Southern Mississippi. He has published over 40 books including 14 collections of poetry, the most recent being *Americorona* (Wipf & Stock, 2021).

Lynette Lamp is a practicing family physician and recent graduate of the Spalding University MFA program. She has had previous poems published in *JAMA (Journal of American Medical Association), The Pharos,* and *Annals of Internal Medicine.* Lynette lives in Winona, Minnesota.

Haro Lee is a Korean poet who teaches English in South Korea. Her work has been published and is forthcoming in *Michigan Quarterly Review, Zone 3 Press, The Offing, The Indianapolis Review, The Texas Review, Anhinga Press, RHINO Poetry, Dryland Lit,* and *Ghost City Press,* among others. She was also the recipient of *Epiphany Magazine's* Breakout 8 Writers Prize.

Bruce Levine has spent his life as a writer of fiction and poetry and as a music and theatre professional. A 2019 *Pushcart Prize* Poetry nominee, a 2021 *Spillwords Press Awards* winner, the *Featured Writer* in WestWard Quarterly Summer 2021 and his bio is featured in *"Who's Who of Emerging Writers 2020."* Bruce has over three hundred works published on over twenty-five on-line journals including *Ariel Chart, Spillwords, The Drabble*; in over seventy print books including *Poetry Quarterly, Haiku Journal, Tipton Poetry Journal; Halcyon Days Founder's Favourites* (on-line and print) and his shows have been produced in New York and around the country. His work is dedicated to the loving memory of his late wife, Lydia Franklin. A native Manhattanite, Bruce now lives and writes in Maine. Visit him at brucelevine.com.

Paul Lojeski was born and raised in Lakewood, Ohio. He attended Oberlin College. His poetry has appeared online and in print. He lives in Port Jefferson, New York.
Poet and filmmaker

Dave Malone lives in the Missouri Ozarks. His latest poetry volume is *Tornado Drill* (Aldrich Press, 2022), and his poems have appeared in *Plainsongs, San Pedro River Review,* and *Delta Poetry Review*. He can be found online at davemalone.net or via Instagram @dave.malone.

Tara Menon is an Indian-American writer based in Lexington, Massachusetts. Her latest fiction has appeared or is forthcoming in *The Hong Kong Review, Litro, The Bookends Review, Rio Grande Review,* and *The Evening Street Review*. Her most recent poems have been published or are forthcoming in *Arlington Literary Journal, Global South, San Pedro River Review, The Loch Raven Review,* and *The Tiger Moth Review*. She is also a book reviewer and essayist whose pieces have appeared in many journals.

Karla Linn Merrifield lives in Florida and has 16 books to her credit. Her newest poetry collection, *My Body the Guitar*, recently nominated for the National Book Award, was inspired by famous guitarists and their guitars and published in December 2021 by Before Your Quiet Eyes Publications Holograph Series (Rochester, NY). She is a frequent contributor to *The Songs of Eretz Poetry Review*. Web site: https://www.karlalinnmerrifield.org/; blog at https://karlalinnmerrifield.wordpress.com/; Tweet @LinnMerrifiel; https://www.facebook.com/karlalinn.merrifield.

Nancy Huxtable Mohr is a retired teacher. Her work explores motherhood, embodiment, the climate crisis, and nature. She lives part-time in Northern California and Upstate New York. She considers herself a farm girl although it's been a long time since she milked a cow. Her work can be found in many journals, most recently in *Cider Press Review, BeZine, Concho River Review, Avocet, Rogue Agent,* and others. More of her work can be found on her website at www.nancyhuxtablemohr.org and Instagram @nancy.mohr

Cameron Morse is Senior Reviews editor at *Harbor Review* and the author of eight collections of poetry. His first collection, *Fall Risk*, won Glass Lyre Press's 2018 Best Book Award. His book of unrhymed sonnets, *Sonnetizer*, is forthcoming from Kelsay Books. He holds an MFA from the University of Kansas City-Missouri and lives in Independence, Missouri, with his wife Lili and three children. For more information, check out his Facebook page or website.

Saraswati Nagpal is an Indian writer and poet, a lover of fantasy and sci-fi. Her graphic novels '*Sita, Daughter of the Earth*' and '*Draupadi, the Fire-born Princess*' are retellings of epic Indian myths in the female voice. Her poetry has appeared in *Cathexis Northwest Press* and *The Journal of Radical Wonder*. She is also a classical dancer who choreographs and performs for film and stage. When she isn't writing, she attempts to inspire teenagers by teaching literature. Twitter: @SaraswatiNagpal / Insta: @saraswatinagpal

Thomas Alan Orr's most recent collection is *Tongue to the Anvil: New and Selected Poems* (Restoration Press). His work has appeared in numerous journals. He works for a community development organization in Indianapolis and lives on a small farm in Shelby County where he raises Flemish Giant rabbits.

A native of Indianapolis, **Tawn Parent** has been a professional writer and editor for 30 years. She has worked primarily for business publications and also served as proofreader for two books. She holds a B.A. in journalism and French from Indiana University and a master's degree in English language acquisition from Marian University. She is working on a compilation of poems about her young son's cancer journey.

Born in the Caribbean and raised in the U.S., **Tia Paul-Louis** began writing songs at age 11, then experimented with poetry during high school. She earned a BA in English/Creative Writing from the University of South Florida along with a M.F.A in Creative Writing from National University in California. Her works have appeared in literary magazines such as *The Voices Project, Ethos Literary Journal,* and *Rabbit Catastrophe Review*. Some of her favorite authors and poets include Langston Hughes, Emily Dickinson, Maya Angelou and Edgar Allan Poe. Apart from writing, Paul-Louis enjoys music, photography, acting and cooking, though she mostly finds herself and others through poetry. She currently lives in Georgia.

Timothy Pilgrim, Montana native and Pacific Northwest poet, has a few hundred acceptances from U.S. journals such as *Seattle Review, San Pedro River Review, Tipton Poetry Journal,* and *Santa Ana River Review*, and international journals such as *Windsor Review* and *Toasted Cheese* in Canada, *Prole Press* in the United Kingdom, and *Otoliths* in Australia. He is the author of *Seduced by metaphor* (2021). He now lives in Washington state.

Ken Poyner lives in Norfolk, Virginia. This year he has published several pieces of microfiction and between twenty and thirty poems, three of which have been nominated for a Pushcart Prize.

Recent work by **Bruce Robinson** appears or is forthcoming in *Tar River Poetry, Spoon River, Rattle, Mantis, Two Hawks Quarterly, Peregrine, Tipton Poetry Journal, North Dakota Quarterly,* and *Aji*. He lives in Brooklyn, New York.

Mykyta Ryzhykh lives in Ukraine and was a finalist of the Crimean fig competition and 2022 Pushcart Nominee (*Tipton Poetry Journal*). Mykyta has been published in the journals *White Mammoth, Soloneba, Littsentr, Plumbum Press, Ukrainian Literary Gazette, Bukovynskyi Journal, Stone Poetry Journal, Tipton Poetry Journal, Alternate route, dyst journal, Better than Starbucks poetry & Fiction Journal, Allegro Poetry Magazine, Littoral Press, Asorn haiku Journal, Book of Matches, Ice Floe Press*.and *Literary Chernihiv*.

Richard Schiffman is an environmental reporter, poet and author of two biographies based in New York City. His poems have appeared on the BBC and on NPR as well as in *Alaska Quarterly, New Ohio Review, Christian Science Monitor, New York Times, Writer's Almanac, This American Life in Poetry, Verse Daily* and other publications. His first poetry collection *What the Dust Doesn't Know* was published in 2017 by Salmon Poetry

R L Swihart was born in Michigan but now resides in Long Beach California. His work has sparsely dotted both the Net and hardcopy literary journals (*Cordite, Pif Magazine, The Literary Bohemian, Offcourse, Otoliths, Denver Quarterly, Quadrant Magazine, The Bookends Review*). His third book of poetry was released July 2020: *Woodhenge*.

Eugene Stevenson , son of immigrants, father of expatriates, lives in the Smoky Mountains of North Carolina. Eisenhower Fellow, Pushcart Prize nominee & author of *The Population of Dreams* (Finishing Line Press 2022), his poems have appeared *in* The *Galway Review, The Hudson Review, San Pedro River Review, Third Wednesday, Tipton Poetry Journal* & *Washington Square Review* among others

Gene Twaronite is the author of four collections of poetry as well as the rhyming picture book *How to Eat Breakfast*. His first poetry book *Trash Picker on Mars*, published by Kelsay Books, was the winner of the 2017 New Mexico-Arizona Book Award for Arizona poetry. His newest poetry collection *Shopping Cart Dreams* will be published by Kelsay Books in 2022. Gene's poems have been described as: "ranging from edgy to whimsical to inscrutable ... playfully haunting and hauntingly playful." A former New Englander, Gene now lives in Tucson. Follow more of his poetry at genetwaronite.poet.com or https://www.instagram.com/genetwaronitepoetry/.

Sophia Upshaw lives in Tallahassee, Florida. Her work has been featured in *The Kudzu Review* and *Mistake House Magazine*.

Mark Vogel lives at the back of a Blue Ridge holler with his wife, Susan Weinberg, an accomplished fiction and creative non-fiction writer, and two foster sons. He currently is an Emeritus Professor of English at Appalachian State University in Boone, North Carolina. Poems and short stories have appeared in several dozen literary journals.

Alessio Zanelli is an Italian poet who writes in English and whose work has appeared in over 200 literary journals from 16 countries. His fifth original collection, titled *The Secret Of Archery*, was published in 2019 by Greenwich Exchange Publishing (London). For more information please visit www.alessiozanelli.it.

Editor

Barry Harris is editor of the *Tipton Poetry Journal* and four anthologies by Brick Street Poetry: *Mapping the Muse: A Bicentennial Look at Indiana Poetry; Words and Other Wild Things* and *Cowboys & Cocktails:Poems from the True Grit Saloon,* and *Reflections on Little Eagle Creek.* He has published one poetry collection, *Something At The Center.*

Married and father of two grown sons, Barry lives in Brownsburg, Indiana and is retired from Eli Lilly and Company.

His poetry has appeared in *Kentucky Review, Valparaiso Poetry Review, Grey Sparrow, Silk Road Review, Saint Ann's Review, North Dakota Quarterly, Boston Literary Magazine, Night Train, Silver Birch Press, Flying Island, Awaken Consciousness, Writers' Bloc, Red-Headed Stepchild* and *Laureate: The Literary Journal of Arts for Lawrence.* One of his poems was on display at the National Museum of Sport and another is painted on a barn in Boone County, Indiana as part of Brick Street Poetry's Word Hunger public art project. His poems are also included in these anthologies: *From the Edge of the Prairie; Motif 3: All the Livelong Day;* and *Twin Muses: Art and Poetry.*

He graduated a long time ago with a major in English from Ball State University.

Made in United States
Orlando, FL
13 January 2023

28630314R00043